Fast Reference Guide to Using dBASE II®

John D. McCharen
MicroComputer Education, Inc.

HAYDEN BOOK COMPANY, INC.
Hasbrouck Heights, New Jersey

This quick reference guide is one of a two-volume set for dBASE II. A fast reference to all dBASE II functions and commands is included in this volume. A detailed reference is provided only for those commands which are commonly invoked from the terminal. A detailed reference for dBASE II functions and those commands more commonly invoked from within command files is found in the **FAST REFERENCE GUIDE TO PROGRAMMING dBASE II**

Acquisitions Editor: DOUGLAS McCORMICK
Production Editor: MAUREEN CONNELLY
Art Director: JIM BERNARD
Composition: ART, COPY, AND PRINT, INC.
Printed and bound by: COMMAND WEB OFFSET, INC.

Printed in the United States of America

1	2	3	4	5	6	7	8	9	PRINTING
84	85	86	87	88	89	90	91	92	YEAR

Files

dBASE II filenames are 1 to 8 characters optionally prefixed by a disk drive and optionally suffixed by a filetype.

The optional drive letter followed by a colon (:) is the letter of the drive where the file resides. If it is not specified, the dBASE II **DEFAULT** drive is assumed. If the filetype is not specified by the user, dBASE II assumes it to be one of the following:

.DBF — database file
.MEM — memory file
.CMD — command file
.FRM — report form file
.TXT — text output file
.NDX — index file
.FMT — format file

Command Format Notation

[ ] Brackets:

Items within square brackets are optional.

< > Braces:

Items within pointed braces are variables supplied by the user.

boldface:

Items in boldface are keywords which are written as shown.

Variables and Constants (or Literals)

dBASE II supports three types of variables and constants:

- character

- numeric
- logical or boolean

Variables are specified by database field names or memory variable names.

Character constants are specified as a character string enclosed in single quotes (') or double quotes (").

Numeric constants are specified with an optional sign, decimal digits, and an optional decimal point.

Boolean constants are represented by T, t, Y, y for true, and by F, f, N, n for false.

Arithmetic Operators

+	addition
-	subtraction
*	multiplication
/	division

Boolean Operators

.OR.	boolean or
.AND.	boolean and
.NOT.	boolean negation

Character String Operators

+	string concatenation
–	string concatenation with the removal of blanks

Relational Operators

<	less than
>	greater than

=	equal to
#	not equal to
<=	less than or equal to
>=	greater than or equal to
$	a substring of

Expressions

dBASE II supports logical, numeric, and character expressions. Expressions are formed with literals, variables, functions, and the appropriate operators.

Macro Substitution

An ampersand (&) followed by a character string memory variable is replaced by the contents of the variable. The memory variable may be terminated by a period (.) to remove any ambiguity.

Full-Screen Operations—Normal

CTRL-E,A	moves cursor to the previous field
CTRL-X,F	moves cursor to the next field
CTRL-S	moves cursor to previous character
CTRL-D	moves cursor to next character
CTRL-Y	clears the current field
CTRL-V	toggles between replace and insert mode
CTRL-G	deletes the character at the cursor
DEL	deletes the character prior to the cursor
CTRL-Q	quits full-screen editing

Full-Screen Operations—with Browse

CTRL-Z	shifts the screen left one field

CTRL-B	shifts the screen right one field
CTRL-R	moves the cursor up one record
CTRL-C	moves the cursor down one record
CTRL-U	marks/unmarks the current record for deletion
CTRL-Q	exits without saving any changes
CTRL-W	exits and writes the changes to disk

Full-Screen Operations—with Modify

CTRL-N	inserts a blank line at the cursor position
CTRL-T	deletes a line at the cursor position
CTRL-C	scrolls up
CTRL-R	scrolls down
CTRL-W	exits and writes the changes to disk
CTRL-Q	exits without saving any changes

Full-Screen Operations—with Edit

CTRL-U	marks/unmarks the record for deletion
CTRL-R	writes current record and positions to previous record
CTRL-C	writes current record and positions to next record
CTRL-W	writes current record and exits

Full Screen Operations —with Append, Create, Insert

CTRL-C,R	writes the current record to disk and proceeds to the next
<Carriage Return>	terminates operation when cursor is in initial position and no changes have been made

The Functions—Fast Reference

#

returns the current position.

$(<character expression>,<start>,<length>**)**

returns a substring of the given character expression.

*****

returns logical true if the current record has been marked for deletion.

@(<character expression 1>,<character expression 2>**)**

returns an integer representing the location of the first occurrence of the first string in the second, or 0.

!(<character expression>**)**

converts the character string expression to uppercase.

CHR(<numeric expression>**)**

converts the numeric expression to the ASCII character equivalent.

DATE()

returns the system date in the form mm/dd/yy.

EOF

returns logical true if end of file exists.

FILE(<character expression>**)**

returns logical true if the character string exists in the directory.

INT(<numeric expression>**)**

returns the greatest integer value.

LEN(<character expression>**)**

returns the length of a character string.

STR(<numeric expression>,<length>[,<precision>]**)**

returns a character string representing the numeric expression.

TRIM(<character expression>**)**

removes trailing blanks from the character string expression.

VAL(<character expression>**)**

returns an integer from the character string made up of a sign digit and up to one decimal point.

TYPE(<expression>**)**

returns the type of expression: numeric, character, or boolean.

The Commands—Fast Reference

?

Displays the value(s) of a list of expressions.

@

Displays formatted information on the screen or printer. In conjunction with its options and other commands, it is useful for conversing with the terminal.

ACCEPT

Accepts a character string from the terminal and assigns it to a memory variable.

APPEND

Appends records to the database in use. The data may be entered from the terminal or extracted from another file or database.

BROWSE

Allows "browsing" through the database. Data from up to nineteen records at a time is displayed on the screen with forward and backward scrolling permitted. Selected data may be edited.

CANCEL

Cancel the execution of a command file.

CHANGE

Allows the change of selected fields from selected records of the database in use.

CLEAR

Either clears outstanding **GET**s used in conjunction with the **@** command, or resets dBASE II. In the latter case, all databases in use are closed, all memory variables are released, and the primary work area is selected.

CONTINUE

Continues the search initiated by the **LOCATE** command.

COPY

Copies a database to another database or unloads the database to a file in the system data format. In the latter case, the fields of the records may or may not be delimited as desired.

COUNT

Counts selected records of the database in use.

CREATE

Creates a database structure. Data may or may not be entered at the time of creation.

DELETE

Marks selected records for deletion. The records may then be physically deleted with a **PACK** command or may be recovered with a **RECALL** command. Alternatively, an entire file may be deleted.

DISPLAY

Displays selected records from the database in use, or the structure of the database in use, or the contents of all memory variables, or the names of files on the default disk.

DO

Used to execute a command file and to implement the "do while" or "case" constructs within a command file.

EDIT

Allows for the editing of selected fields of the data base.

EJECT

Issues a form feed to the printer when used in conjunction with various print operations.

ENDCASE

Marks the end of the "case" construct.

ENDDO

Marks the end of a "do while" construct.

ENDIF

Marks the end of an "if ... else" construct.

ERASE

Clears the screen and positions the cursor to upper corner of the screen. Also clears memory of any prior **@** command gets and pictures.

FIND

Finds the first occurrence of a record having a given key in an indexed data base.

GO
GOTO

Changes the current position in the database to a specified location.

IF

Used to implement the "if ... else" construct.

INDEX

Creates an index on a specified key for the database in use.

INPUT

Prompts for input from the terminal to a specified memory variable.

INSERT

Inserts a record into the database in use.

JOIN

Creates a "join" of the primary and secondary databases. (See the detailed reference for a description of *join*).

LIST

Lists the records of the database in use, or the structure of the data base in use, or the contents of all memory variables, or files in the directory.

LOCATE

Locates a specified record in the data base. May be used in conjunction with the **CONTINUE** command.

LOOP

Used from within a **DO WHILE** loop to cause control to be passed to the **DO WHILE**.

MODIFY

Allows for the modification of a database structure or a command file.

NOTE
*

Denotes a comment within a command file. An asterisk (*) may also be used.

PACK

Removes records marked for deletion by the **DELETE** command. These records are not recoverable.

QUIT

Closes all files and returns control to the operating system.

READ

Reads data from the terminal as specified by the **GET** phrase within previously issued **@** commands. Full-screen editing is allowed.

RECALL

Recovers records which have been marked for deletion by the **DELETE** command.

RELEASE

Releases selected memory variables.

REMARK

Echoes comments to the screen during the execution of a command file.

RENAME

Renames a file within the directory.

REPLACE

Replaces data within specified portions of the database.

REPORT

Creates a report form or invokes a previously created form. This is a quick way of producing simple reports without creating a command file.

RETURN

Exits a command file returning control to the invoking command file or to the terminal, if the command file was invoked directly from the terminal.

RESTORE

Reads a memory file previously saved with a **SAVE** command. The variables within this file become the current memory variables.

SAVE

Writes the current memory variables to a memory file. This file may be subsequently read by issuing a **RESTORE** command.

SELECT

Allows the user to select a primary or a secondary database for use in subsequent commands.

SET

Sets the selected dBASE II switch **ON** or **OFF**. It is also used to set other global variables.

SKIP

Skips forward or backward through the database; i.e., changes current position.

SORT

Produces a sorted copy of a database on a given field.

STORE

Stores a value in a specified memory variable.

SUM

Sums selected fields from the database in use.

TOTAL

Computes subtotals and places them in a database.

UPDATE

Updates selected records from the database in use with data of another database.

USE

Specifies the database to be used and any associated index files.

WAIT

Waits until a single character is entered from the keyboard.

The Commands—Detailed Reference

? <expression list>

Evaluates a list of expressions. The expressions may be logical, numeric, or character.

where: **<expression list>** is a list of expressions separated by commas.

examples: **? NAME**

will display the contents of the **NAME** field of the current record of the database in use.

? NAME,ADDRESS

will display the contents of the **NAME** and **ADDRESS** fields of the current record of the database in use.

? 2+3

will display 5.

? #

will display the current record number of the database in use.

APPEND

APPEND FROM <file> **[FOR** <expression>**] [SDF]**
[DELIMITED WITH <delimiter>**]**

APPEND BLANK

Appends records to the database in use. When issued with no parameters, the user is prompted to enter the data from the keyboard.

where: **FROM <file>** indicates a file or database from which to take the data. In the absence of the **SDF** and **DELIMITED WITH** phrases, the file is assumed to be a database.

FOR <**expression**> defines the records which will be appended to the database. For each record in the **FROM <file>** a database record is constructed. If <**expression**> is true it is appended. Otherwise it is discarded. If omitted, all records from the **FROM <file>** are appended.

SDF indicates that the **FROM <file>** is in System Data Format.

DELIMITED WITH <delimiter> indicates that the fields within the **FROM <file>** are delimited with **<delimiter>** and separated by commas. If this phrase is used, it is assumed that the **FROM <file>** is in system data format, so **SDF** need not be specified.

*****Special Note*** WITH <delimiter>** is not supported with some versions of dBASE II. In this case, the phrase may be omitted if the **FROM <file>** is delimited by single or double quotes. See the example below.

BLANK causes a space-filled record to be appended to the database. This may subsequently be filled in with other commands.

In addition to the normal full-screen control operations (CTRL-key), the following functions are also supported.

CTRL-C,R Writes the current record to disk and proceeds to the next.

<Carriage Return> Terminates operation when cursor is in initial position and no changes have been made

examples: **APPEND FROM CUSTFILE FOR AMNT:OWED>100.00**

Appends those records from a database named **CUSTFILE** for which the **AMNT:OWED** field is greater than **100.00**.

APPEND FROM CUSTFILE FOR AMNT:OWED>100.00 SDF

Does the same as the previous example except that **CUSTFILE** must be in system data format.

APPEND FROM CUSTFILE DELIMITED

Appends all records from the file named **CUSTFILE**. **CUSTFILE** must be in system data format (because the **DELIMITED** phrase is used) and the fields within this file are delimited with quotes (') or double quotes (") and separated with commas.

BROWSE

This allows perusal of the database and certain editing operations. Initially, records from current position are displayed on the screen. As many fields of each record as will fit are displayed. In addition to the normal full-screen control operations (CTRL-key), the following functions are also supported:

CTRL-Z shifts the screen left one field
CTRL-B shifts the screen right one field
CTRL-R moves the cursor up one record
CTRL-C moves the cursor down one record
CTRL-U marks/unmarks the current record for deletion

CTRL-Q exits without saving any changes
CTRL-W exits and writes the changes to disk

CHANGE [<scope>] FIELD <list> [FOR <expression>]

Changes selected fields from selected records of the database in use. The user is prompted for the changes.

where: **<scope>** defines the scope of the search. **ALL**, **NEXT n**, or **RECORD n** may be written. The default is the current record.

FIELD <list> defines the list of fields to be changed. **<list>** is a list of field names separated by commas.

FOR <expression> defines those records within the scope of the operation presented to the user for change.

examples: **CHANGE FIELD STREET,CITY,ZIP FOR LAST:NAME='Smith'**

Prompts the user to change the **STREET**, **CITY**, and **ZIP** fields for the record whose **LAST:NAME** field contains **Smith**.

LOCATE FOR LAST:NAME='Smith'
CHANGE FIELD STATUS

Prompts the user to change the **STATUS** field of the current record. The database was positioned to the record for **Smith** by the **LOCATE** command.

CONTINUE

Continues the search initiated by a previously issued **LOCATE** or **CONTINUE** statement.

examples: **LOCATE FOR STATE='IL'**

Positions the database to the first record whose **STATE** field is **IL**.

CONTINUE

Positions the database to the next record whose **STATE** field contains **IL**, if issued after the previous **LOCATE** command.

COPY TO <file> **[**<scope>**] [FIELD** <list>**] (FOR** <expression>**]**
[SDF] [STRUCTURE] [DELIMITED [WITH <delimiter>**]]**

Copies the database in use or its structure to a specified file.

where: **TO <file>** designates the receiving file.

<scope> denotes the scope of the operation. **ALL**, **NEXT n**, or **RECORD n** may be written. The default is **ALL**.

FIELD <list> designates the fields which participate in the copy operation. **<list>** is a list of field names separated by commas. The default is all fields.

FOR <expression> defines the records within the scope of the operation that will participate in the copy operation.

SDF indicates that the receiving file is in Standard Data Format. If omitted, a database is assumed (unless **DELIMITED** is coded, in which case a Standard Data Format is assumed).

STRUCTURE indicates that only the database structure is copied. If **STRUCTURE** is written with **FIELD <list>**, then only that portion of the structure indicated by **<list>** is copied.

DELIMITED indicates that the receiving file is in Standard Data Format and the fields will be separated by commas. In the absence of the **WITH <delimiter>** phrase, the fields are delimited with single quotes (').

WITH <delimiter> specifies that the single character **<delimiter>** will be used to delimit the fields within a record. If a comma is used, then character fields will have trailing blanks removed and numeric fields will have leading blanks removed. The default is a single quote.

examples: **COPY TO LABELS FIELD NAME,STREET, CITY,STATE,ZIP DELIMITED WITH "**

Copies the **NAME**, **STREET**, **CITY**, **STATE**, and **ZIP** field to a file named **LABELS**. The file **LABELS** will be in system data format because the **DELIMITED WITH** phrase is used. The fields within each record of the file will be delimited with quotes (") and separated by commas. A typical record in the file might appear as follows:

"Johnny Mercer ","315 Regal ","Sycamore","IL","60178"

COPY TO CUSTFILE FOR AMNT:OWED>100.00

Extracts those records from the database in use whose **AMNT:OWED** field exceeds **100.00** and puts them in a database named **CUSTFILE**.

COUNT [<scope>] [FOR <expression>**] [TO** <memory variable>**]**

Counts records within the database in use.

where: <**scope**> defines the scope of the counting operation. **ALL**, **NEXT n**, or **RECORD n** may be written. **ALL** is the default.

FOR <**expression**> defines the records within the scope of the counting operation which are to be counted. If omitted, each record within the scope of the operation is counted.

TO <**memory variable**> indicates that the result is placed in the designated memory variable.

examples:

COUNT FOR ZIP:CODE='60178' TO NUMZIP

Counts those records for which the field **ZIP:CODE** contains **60178** and places the answer in the memory variable **NUMZIP**. (Here **ZIP:CODE** is a character field.)

CREATE [<file>**]**

Defines a database structure, i.e., creates a database.

where: <**file**> designates the name of the database.

In addition to the normal full-screen control

operations (CTRL-key), the following functions are also supported.

CTRL-C,R	Writes the current record to disk and proceeds to the next.
<Carriage Return>	Terminates operation when cursor is in initial position and no changes have been made

notes: For each field, the user is prompted to enter the name of the field, the type of field (**C**—character, **N**—numeric, **L**—logical), the width of the field, and the number of decimal places for numeric fields.

examples: **. CREATE CUSTOMER**

ENTER RECORD STRUCTURE AS FOLLOWS:

FIELD	NAME,TYPE,WIDTH,DECIMAL PLACES
001	NAME,C,20
002	BALANCE,N,9,2

The above defines a structure for a database having two fields, **NAME** and **BALANCE**. **NAME** is a character field of width **20**. **BALANCE** is a numeric field of width **9**—*including the decimal point*—and containing **2** places beyond the decimal point.

DELETE [<scope>] **[FOR** <expression>**]**
DELETE FILE <file>

Marks selected records for deletion or deletes a file. In the former case, the records may be recovered prior to issuing a **PACK** by issuing a **RECALL** command.

where: **<scope>** defines the scope of the operation. **ALL**, **NEXT n**, or **RECORD n** may be written. The default is the current record.

FOR <expression> defines the records within the scope of the operation that will be marked.

FILE <file> designates a file to be deleted.

examples: **DELETE ALL FOR STATUS='E'**

Marks those records whose **STATUS** field contains **E** for deletion.

DELETE ALL FOR STATUS='E'
RECALL ALL

Gets them back.

DELETE ALL FOR STATUS='E'
PACK

Actually gets rid of them.

DISPLAY [<scope>] **[FOR** <expression>**]** **[**<expression list>**]**
[OFF]
DISPLAY STRUCTURE
DISPLAY MEMORY
DISPLAY FILES [ON <disk drive>**] [LIKE** <skeleton>**]**

Displays the specified information.

where: <**scope**> defines the scope of the operation. **ALL**, **NEXT n**, and **RECORD n** may be specified. In the absence of the **FOR** <**expression**>, the current record is the default. In the presence of the **FOR** <**expression**>, phrase **ALL** is the default.

FOR <**expression**> defines the records within the scope of the operation that will participate in the display.

<**expression list**> is the list of expressions that will be displayed. If this list is omitted, all fields within the record will be displayed.

OFF causes record numbers to be suppressed. If not written, record numbers will be displayed.

STRUCTURE indicates that the database structure is to be displayed.

MEMORY indicates that all memory variables are to be displayed.

FILES indicates that a list of files on either the specified or default drive is to be displayed.

ON <**disk drive**> indicates the drive where the files are to reside. <**disk drive**> is written as **x**: where "x" is the letter denoting the drive. The dBASE II **DEFAULT** drive is the default value.

LIKE <skeleton> indicates which files are to be displayed. If the phrase is omitted, all files on the specified drive are displayed. Otherwise only those files that "match" the **<skeleton>** are display.

examples: **DISPLAY FOR AMOUNT>100.00 NAME,STREET,CITY,STATE,ZIP**

Displays the **NAME**, **STREET**, **CITY**, **STATE**, and **ZIP** fields for those records having an **AMOUNT** field greater than **100.00**.

DISPLAY FILES ON B: LIKE *.dbf

Displays those files having a file type "dbf".

EDIT [<n>]

Allows editing of selected fields of selected records of the database in use.

where: **<n>** is the record number of the record to be edited. If it is omitted, the user is prompted for the number.

In addition to the normal full-screen control operations (CTRL-key), the following functions are also supported.

CTRL-U	marks/unmarks the record for deletion
CTRL-R	writes current record and positions to previous record
CTRL-C	writes current record and positions to next record
CTRL-W	writes current record and exits

notes: If not in full-screen mode, the user is prompted to enter the record number, the field name, and the new contents of the field.

FIND <key>

Sets current position to the first record of the database in use whose key is equal to the specified key.

where: **<key>** defines the key for the search.

notes: The database must be used with the **INDEX**ed option.

example: **USE CUSTOMER INDEX CUSTNDX**
FIND 'Smith'

Positions to the first record of the database whose key is **Smith**. The key for the index is a character expression, and thus the key was enclosed in quotes here.

SET INDEX TO CUSTNDX2
FIND 100

Positions to the first record of the database whose key is **100**. The key for the index is a numeric expression in this case.

GO TOP
GO BOTTOM
GO <n>
GO <memory variable>

Positions to the specified record within the database.

where: **TOP** specifies the first record of the database.

BOTTOM specifies the last record of the database.

<**n**> specifies the "nth" record of the database.

<**memory variable**> specifies the record in the database indicated by the contents of the indicated memory variable.

notes: **GO** may be written as **GOTO**, <**n**> may be written as **RECORD** <**n**>, **GO** <**n**> may be written as <**n**>

INDEX ON <expression> TO <index>

Creates an index to the database in use on the specified expression.

where: <**expression**> is the expression upon which the index is formed. It is known as the **key** for the index.

<**index**> is the name of the index file to be created.

examples: **INDEX ON LAST:NAME TO NDXFILE1**

Creates an index file named **NDXFILE1** keyed on the **LAST:NAME** field of the database in use.

INDEX ON LAST:NAME+FIRST:NAME TO NDXFILE2

Creates an index file named **NDXFILE2** keyed on the concatenation of the **LAST:NAME** and **FIRST:NAME** fields of the database in use.

INSERT [BEFORE] [BLANK]

Inserts a record into the database in use.

where: **BEFORE** indicates that the record is to be inserted before the current record. If not specified, the record is inserted after the current record.

BLANK causes a space filled record to be inserted. If not specified, the user is prompted to enter the data.

In addition to the normal full-screen control operations (CTRL-key), the following functions are also supported.

CTRL-C,R Writes the current record to disk and proceeds to the next.

<Carriage Return> Terminates operation when cursor is in initial Return position and no changes have been made

JOIN TO <file> FOR <expression> [FIELDS <field list>]

Creates a "join" of the primary and secondary databases.

where: **TO <file>** specifies the name of the join.

FOR <expression> defines those records participating in the join as described below.

FIELDS <field list> defines the fields for the join. **<field list>** is a list of field names, separated by commas, from the primary and secondary databases. If this phrase is omitted, then all fields from the primary database, and as many fields as possible from the secondary database (to a maximum of 32) are used. A field name may be prefixed with a **P.** or an **S.** to indicate whether it is in the primary or secondary database, respectively.

notes: The join of the two databases is created by evaluating <**expression**> for each pair of records from the primary and secondary databases. For each pair for which the expression is true, a record is added to the joined database.

The pairs are examined by cycling through the secondary database for each record in the primary database.

A **SELECT PRIMARY** command must be issued prior to issuing the **JOIN** command.

examples: **SELECT PRIMARY**
USE CUSTFILE
SELECT SECONDARY
USE ACCTFILE
SELECT PRIMARY
JOIN RPTFILE FOR P.ACCT:NUM =S.ACCT:NUM FIELDS P.NAME, P.ADDRESS,S.BALANCE

Creates a join of the **CUSTFILE** and **ACCTFILE** databases. For each pair of records in these databases having the same **ACCT:NUM** fields, a record is constructed for the **RPTFILE** database consisting of the **NAME** and **ADDRESS** field from the primary database, and the **BALANCE** field of the **SECONDARY** database.

LIST [<scope>**] [FOR** <expression>**] [**<expression list>**] [OFF]**
LIST STRUCTURE
LIST MEMORY
LIST FILES [ON <disk drive>**] [LIKE** <skeleton>**]**

LIST is the same as **DISPLAY** except that there is no pause after record groups, and <**scope**> defaults to **ALL**.

examples: **LIST NEXT 10 FOR LAST:NAME='Smith'**

Lists those records out of the next 10 records whose **LAST:NAME** field is **Smith**.

LOCATE [<scope>**] [FOR** <expression>**]**

Positions the database to the first record for which the expression is true.

where: <**scope**> defines the scope of the search operation. **ALL**, **NEXT n**, or **RECORD n** may be written. ALL is the default.

FOR <**expression**> defines those records which can satisfy the search. The database is positioned on the first record within the scope of the operation for which the expression is true. If no record is found, the database is positioned on the last record scanned.

notes: The search may be continued from the current position with the **CONTINUE** command.

examples: **LOCATE FOR AMOUNT>100.00.AND.MONTHS>6**

Positions to the first record of the database in use having an **AMOUNT** field greater than **100.00** and a **MONTHS** field greater than **6**.

CONTINUE will continue the search and position to the next record satisfying the specified criteria.

MODIFY STRUCTURE

Deletes all database records and provides full-screen editing of the structure in use. In addition to the normal full-screen control operations (CTRL-key), the following functions are also supported:

CTRL-N	inserts a blank line at the cursor position
CTRL-T	deletes a line at the cursor position
CTRL-C	scrolls up
CTRL-R	scrolls down
CTRL-W	exits and writes the changes to disk
CTRL-Q	exits without saving any changes

notes: To modify a structure and save the records, the database must be copied to a temporary database and then appended to the modified structure.

PACK

Physically deletes all records marked for deletion within the database in use. Any index files in use are updated.

QUIT [TO <command list>**]**

Closes all files and returns to the operating system. Optionally, a list of system commands may be executed upon exit.

where: <**command list**> is a list of system commands to be executed upon exit. Commands are enclosed in quotes and separated by commas.

examples: **QUIT TO 'DIR B:','STAT B:','DBASE'**

This closes files, displays the directory on the b: drive, shows the status on the b: drive, and returns to dBASE II.

RECALL [<scope>] **[FOR** <expression>**]**

Recovers records within the scope of the operation which were marked for deletion by the **DELETE** command.

where: <**scope**> defines the scope of the operation. **ALL**, **NEXT n**, and **RECORD n** may be coded. **ALL** is the default in the presence of **FOR** <**expression**>. Otherwise the current record is recovered.

FOR <**expression**> defines those records within the scope of the operation that are recovered.

examples: **RECALL FOR STATUS='PAID'**

Recovers those records having a **STATUS** field of **PAID**.

RENAME <old file name> **TO** <new file name>

Renames a file in the system directory.

where: <**old file name**> is the original name of the file.

<**new file name**> is the new name of the file.

notes: If a filetype is not specified, dBASE II will assume a filetype of .DBF.

If the drive is not specified, the default drive is assumed.

example: **RENAME RPTFILE.BAK TO RPTFILE.FRM**

Renames the backup file **RPTFILE.BAK**, which resides on the default drive.

RENAME B:NDXFILE.BAK TO NDXFILE.NDX

Renames the backup file **NDXFILE.BAK**, which resides on the b: drive.

RENAME CUSTFILE.BAK TO CUSTFILE

Renames the backup file **CUSTFILE.BAK**, which resides on the default drive giving it a new name **CUSTFILE.DBF**.

REPLACE [<scope>**]** <field1> **WITH** <expression1> [,field2> **WITH** <expression2>, **...] [FOR** <expression>**]**

Replaces a field(s) with an expression(s).

where: <**scope**> defines the scope of the operation. **ALL**, **NEXT n**, or **RECORD n** may be written. The current record is the default.

<**field**> **WITH** <**expression**> defines the new contents of a field. <**expression**> will replace the contents of the field having name <field>.

FOR <**expression**> defines those records within the scope of the operation that will be affected.

notes: Any index file in use will be updated if a key field is affected. This will change positions of records within the database and index so **NEXT n** should probably not be used as the scope in this case.

examples: **REPLACE LAST:NAME WITH 'Smith'**

Replaces the **LAST:NAME** field within the current record with **Smith**.

REPLACE ALL STATUS WITH 'OVERDUE' FOR BALANCE>0

Replaces the **STATUS** field with **OVERDUE** in **ALL** records for which the **BALANCE** field is greater than **0**.

REPORT [FORM <file>**] [**<scope>**] [FOR** <expression>**] [TO PRINT] [PLAIN]**

Creates a report **FORM** or "layout" and produces the report. The first time the **REPORT** command is issued, a file is created specifying the layout of the report. Subsequent use of the command specifying this file will generate a report using the data from the database in use.

where: **FORM** <**file**> denotes the name of the file from which the report is produced. If this file does not already exist, the user is prompted to enter the appropriate information to create it.

<**scope**> defines the scope of the records that will participate in the report. **ALL**, **NEXT n**, or **RECORD n** may be written. **ALL** is the default.

FOR <**expression**> defines those records within the scope of the operation that will participate in the report.

TO PRINT directs the report to the printer as well as the screen.

PLAIN causes page numbers and date to be suppressed.

REPORT FORM CUSTRPT

Prompts the user for information to create a form file **CUSTRPT**, if it does not already exist. If it does exist, the report is displayed on the screen.

REPORT FORM CUSTRPT FOR BALANCE <0 TO PRINT

Prints a report defined by the form file **CUSTRPT** using only those records of the database in use having a **BALANCE** field less than **0**.

RESTORE FROM <file>

Restores all memory variables from a previously saved set of memory variables.

where: **FROM** <file> denotes the name of the memory file from which to read the variables

notes: The memory file must be created initially with the **SAVE** command.

SELECT PRIMARY
SELECT SECONDARY

Selects the active database area.

where: **PRIMARY** denotes the primary area.
SECONDARY denotes the secondary area.

notes: dBASE II has two database areas in which databases can be used. Initially, the **PRIMARY** area is active. The database in use in the active area is the object of dBASE II commands.
Fields can be referenced in the primary or secondary databases by a **P.** or a **S.** prefix, respectively. If the prefix is omitted, it is assumed that the reference is for the active area.

examples: **SELECT PRIMARY**
USE DB1
SELECT SECONDARY
USE DB2
SELECT PRIMARY
LIST
SELECT SECONDARY
LIST
The first **LIST** command will list the records from DB1, the second will list records from DB2.

SET <toggle> ON
SET <toggle> OFF
SET <parameter> TO >value>

Sets the values of various dBASE II variables as described below. The defaults are underlined.

<toggle>	action	
ALTERNATE	ON	Output is echoed to a disk file.
	OFF	Output is not echoed to a disk file.
BELL	ON	Bell rings whenever illegal data are entered or data boundaries are crossed.
	OFF	The bell is turned off.
CARRY	ON	Data from previous record will be carried over to the current record when appending records in full-screen mode.
	OFF	No such carrying of data is performed.
COLON	ON	Bounds **GET** data items with colons (:) in **@** commands.
	OFF	Colons are not displayed.
CONFIRM	ON	The cursor will not skip to the next field in full-screen editing until a control key is entered.
	OFF	The cursor will move to the next field when the current field is filled.
CONSOLE	ON	Output is echoed to the screen.
	OFF	Output is not echoed to the screen.
DEBUG	ON	Output from the **ECHO** and **STEP** commands will be sent to the printer.
	OFF	Such output will not be sent to the printer.
ECHO	ON	Commands executed from within a command file are echoed to the terminal.
	OFF	They are not echoed.
EJECT	ON	The **REPORT** command will

		eject a page before printing the report.
	OFF	The eject is suppressed.
ESCAPE	ON	An escape character aborts execution of command files.
	OFF	There is no escape.
EXACT	ON	Requires that character strings match completely in expressions and the **FIND** command.
	OFF	Comparisons are made on the basis of the length of the second operand. Thus "hotdog" = "hot" is true.
INTENSITY	ON	Full-screen operations will use dual-intensity screen characters.
	OFF	Only normal intensity is used.
LINKAGE	ON	Positioning is done for both the primary and secondary databases for sequential commands (i.e., those having a <scope> parameter).
	OFF	Positioning is done independently on the primary and secondary databases.
PRINT	ON	Output is echoed to the printer.
	OFF	Output is not echoed to the printer.
RAW	ON	Spaces are not inserted between fields by the **DISPLAY** and **LIST** commands.
	OFF	Such spaces are inserted.
SCREEN	ON	Full-screen operations are turned on for **APPEND**, **INSERT**, **EDIT**, **DISPLAY**, **MODIFY**, and **CREATE** commands.
	OFF	Full-screen operations are turned off.

<table>
<tr><td>STEP</td><td>ON</td><td>dBASE II pauses after each command executed in a command file to allow the user to enter a command, escape, or resume execution of the command file.</td></tr>
<tr><td></td><td>OFF</td><td>Normal operations are resumed.</td></tr>
<tr><td>TALK</td><td>ON</td><td>Results from commands are displayed on the screen.</td></tr>
<tr><td></td><td>OFF</td><td>There is no display.</td></tr>
</table>

SET HEADING TO <string>

Sets the default heading for reports.

where: **<string>** is a character string up to 60 characters.

SET FORMAT TO [SCREEN] [PRINT] [<format file>]

where: **[SCREEN]** specifies that the output of the **@** command will be directed to the screen.

[PRINT] specifies that the output of the **@** command will be directed to the printer.

<format file> designates the source of data for the **READ** command.

SET DEFAULT TO <drive>

Sets the default disk drive.

where: **<drive>** designates the disk drive. It is written as **x**: or simply **x** where **x** is the drive.

notes: This form of the **SET** command does not affect the system default drive.

SET ALTERNATE TO [<file>]

If the **ALTERNATE** toggle is **ON**, then all data written to the screen or the printer will also be written to the file designated by **<file>**.

SET DATE TO mm/dd/yy

Sets the dBASE II system date.

SET INDEX TO [<index>**[,**<index2>**, ...]]**

Specifies a set of index files to be used in subsequent commands. When no operands are specified, all index files in use are closed.

where: **<index>** denotes the master index. If not specified, then all index files are closed.

SET MARGIN TO <n>

Sets the default margin for reports.

where: **<n>** is an integer in the range 1 to 254.

SKIP[-] [>expression>**]**
[+]

Adjusts the current position in the database forward or backward.

where: – is an optional sign. + may also be coded but is redundant.

<expression> is a numeric expression denoting the number of records to be skipped.

notes: **SKIP** with no parameters moves forward one record.

examples: **SKIP –5**

Sets position back five records in the data base.

SORT ON <field> **TO** <file>**[ASCENDING]**
[DESCENDING]

Sorts the database in use on the specified field.

where: **ON <field>** specifies the field to govern the sort.

TO <file> denotes the destination for the sorted database.

ASCENDING denotes that the database is to be sorted in ascending order.

DESCENDING denotes that the database is to be sorted in descending order.

notes: A database may be sorted on more than one field by cascading **SORT** commands. Sort on the minor key first and progress to the major key.

If neither **ASCENDING** nor **DESCEND-**

ING is written, the file is sorted in ascending order.

examples: **SORT ON LAST:NAME TO ODRFILE ASCENDING**

Sorts the database in use on the **LAST:NAME** field creating the sorted file **ODRFILE**.

STORE <expression> **TO** <memory variable>

Stores the evaluated expression in the designated memory variable.

examples: **STORE AMOUNT+BALANCE TO MVALUE**

Evaluates the sum of the **AMOUNT** and **BALANCE** fields of the database in use and stores the result in a memory variable named **MVALUE**.

SUM <expression1>**[**,<expression2> **...]**
[TO <memory variable list>**]** **[**<scope>**]**
[FOR <expression>**]**

Sums the designated expression for the specified records of the database in use.

where: <**expression1-5**> denotes numeric expressions to be summed. Up to five expressions can be summed.

TO <**memory variable list**> designates memory variables to receive the sums.

<**scope**> defines the scope of the operation. **ALL**, **NEXT n**, or **RECORD n** may be coded. **ALL** is the default.

FOR <expression> defines those records within the scope of the operation which will participate in the summing.

notes: Records which are marked for deletion will not participate in the summing.

examples: **SUM DEPOSITS,WITHDRAWAL TO TOTDEP,TOTWDRW**

Accumulates the sum of the **DEPOSITS** and **WITHDRAWAL** fields of the database in use and places the results in the memory variable fields **TOTDEP** and **TOTWDRW**.

TOTAL ON <key> **TO** <database>**[FIELDS** <list>**]**
[FOR <expression>**]**

Forms subtotals for the given key and places the results in the specified database.

where: **ON** <key> is the key upon which subtotals are performed.

TO <database> is the destination database for the subtotals. It is created with the structure of the database in use if it does not already exist.

FIELDS <list> defines those fields for which subtotals will be accumulated. All numeric fields in the receiving database is the default.

FOR <expression> defines those records which will participate in the accumulations.

notes: If **FIELDS <list>** is not specified, then all numeric fields in the **TO <database>** are accumulated. This implies that they exist in database in use.

The **<key>** field must exist in the **TO <database>**.

examples: **TOTAL ON CUSTID TO STATEMENT FIELDS DEPOSITS,WITHDRAWAL**

Accumulates subtotals of the **DEPOSITS** and **WITHDRAWAL** fields of the database in use for each value of the key **CUSTID** and places these subtotals along with the value of the key in the corresponding fields of the **STATEMENT** database.

UPDATE FROM <database> **ON** <key> **[ADD** <field list>**]**
[REPLACE <field list>**]**

Alters fields in the database in use with data from another database.

where: **FROM <database>** is the source of the update data.

ON <key> defines the key for the update operation.

ADD <field list> defines a list cf fields which are accumulated from the corresponding fields in the **FROM <database>**.

REPLACE <field list> defines a list of fields which are replaced from the corresponding fields **FROM <database>**.

notes: The database in use must be sorted on the <**key**> or indexed on the <**key**>. The **FROM** <**database**> must be sorted on the key.

The keys in the database in use should probably be unique, although no error is flagged if they are not.

examples: **UPDATE FROM SALES ON PARTNUM ADD SALES:AMNT**

Updates the database in use by accumulating the **SALES:AMNT** field from the **SALES** database.

UPDATE FROM CUSTFILE ON CUSTID REPLACE ADDRESS

Updates the database in use by replacing the **ADDRESS** field with data from the **CUSTFILE** database.

USE (<database>) (INDEX <index list>)

Closes the database in use and optionally uses a database into the selected area.

where: <**database**> specifies a database to be used in the selected area.

INDEX <index list> defines a set of index files to be opened. The first file in the list is the master index, which governs those commands which use an index. All index files in this list are updated by the **APPEND, EDIT, REPLACE, READ, BROWSE,** and **PACK** commands.

notes: A maximum of seven index files can be opened at any one time. These files may be closed and another set opened with the SET INDEX TO command.

examples: **USE CUSTOMER INDEX NAMENDX**

Uses the CUSTOMER database with the index file NAMENDX.

USE

Closes the database in use.

Common dBASE II Error Messages

BAD NAME FIELD

The field name supplied does not conform to conventions.

BAD TYPE FIELD

The field type must be **C** for character, **N** for numeric, or **L** for logical type.

BAD DECIMAL WIDTH FIELD or BAD WIDTH FIELD

The width of the field being defined is invalid.

COMMAND FILE CANNOT BE FOUND

The command file does not exist or was misspelled.

DATA ITEM NOT FOUND

The command contains an undefined database field name.

DISK IS FULL

The disk cannot hold any more data.

"FIELD" PHRASE NOT FOUND

See PHRASE ERRORS below.

FILE DOES NOT EXIST

The file name given is not on the disk or is misspelled.

FILE IS CURRENTLY OPEN

Operation requires that the file be closed via USE or CLEAR.

ILLEGAL VARIABLE NAME

The variable name supplied does not conform to conventions.

INDEX FILE CANNOT BE OPENED

Index file name was probably misspelled or does not exist.

MACRO IS NOT A CHARACTER STRING

Macros must be character-type memory variables.

NO "FOR" PHRASE

See PHRASE ERRORS below.

NO "FROM" PHRASE

See PHRASE ERRORS below.

NO FIND

The specified key was not found.

"ON" PHRASE NOT FOUND

See PHRASE ERRORS below.

RECORD NOT IN INDEX

The database was probably updated when the index was not in use. The index will have to be recreated.

RECORD OUT OF RANGE

The record number provided does not exist in the database.

SOURCE AND DESTINATION DATA TYPES ARE DIFFERENT

Attempt to REPLACE a field of one data type with another type of data.

*** SYNTAX ERROR ***

The command given does not conform to the definition.

"TO" PHRASE NOT FOUND

See PHRASE ERRORS below.

"WITH" PHRASE NOT FOUND

See PHRASE ERRORS below.

*** UNKNOWN COMMAND

The command issued is not a dBASE II command.

PHRASE ERRORS

Some commands require certain "phrases" in order to work correctly. If a phrase is missing, an error message is issued stating what type of phrase was expected for the command. The same message may be issued if correct phrases are provided but do not follow the order according to the command definition.

Correcting Erroneous Statements:

dBASE II provides an error correction facility for commands that are incorrect. After the type of error is listed, the correction dialogue might look like the following:

CORRECT AND RETRY (Y/N)?	**Y** allows statement correction.
CHANGE FROM :	A character string with the error is typed.
CHANGE TO :	The correct character string is typed.
MORE CORRECTIONS (Y/N)?	**Y** allows more corrections to the statement.